Interview

How To Best Prepare For An

Interview And Land Your Dream

Job In 2016!

Steve Gold

Table of Contents

Introduction

It is not too much of an exaggeration to think of a job interview as one of the most nerve wrecking situations one can be in. For young job seekers just starting off, it can be a defining moment which – whatever the outcome may be – can have a massive impact on one's self-esteem. For career changers, there's no telling what to expect in the unpredictable job market.

Times have certainly changed, and so have the requirements and expectations of employers; what was acceptable or applicable a few years ago may not be so in the modern age. This also means that hiring practices are no longer the same. Ultimately, when it comes to nailing a job interview, knowledge is power and preparation is key – that will never change. The question then becomes how can one adapt to changing hiring practices and ace a job interview in the current climate? What are the things one should know and how can one be best prepared?

In the following chapters, you will gain a better understanding of the job interview process as well as common interviewing practices that are unique to this particular period in time. You will then be guided on how to best prepare when called for a job interview, from what questions to anticipate and how to best handle the tricky ones in order to give yourself the best possible chance of landing the job. Insights will also begin on making a good first impression the moment you meet the hiring manager.

Getting called for an interview is a golden opportunity afforded only to a handful of hopefuls who apply for a job opening, so you need to make the most out of it.

Good luck!

Chapter 1

The Job Interview Demystified

After sending out numerous job applications and patiently waiting, you've finally got the much anticipated call to go for an interview with a potential employer. Having managed to get a job interview means you have surpassed countless other applicants vying for the job, and are among the shortlisted candidates deemed qualified to fill the position. You are being given the chance to convince a potential employer firsthand that you are the person their organization needs. As such, you want to be sure to make the most out of this golden opportunity by putting your best foot forward and, hopefully, secure the job you want.

Job Interviews: Then vs. Now

In the not-so-distant past, people were oftentimes introduced to job openings through being referred by someone or by browsing the classified advertisements in newspapers. Competition was not as though, and if you were lucky enough to be referred by someone the employer knew and trusted, you were likely to already have an advantage over the other candidates.

However, when the internet became the main outlet for recruitment and job searching in the new millennium, it changed the game. Job applicants began to have easier access to information on who was hiring, leading to a significantly higher responses to job postings. Recruiters were then faced with the overwhelming task of sorting through hundreds, maybe even thousands, of applications and narrowing down potential candidates to a small handful. The selected few would then have to go through a tough interview process until the suitable candidate was found from among the hopefuls.

It is hardly a surprise that recruiters have changed their interviewing practices, and now take a tougher approach when screening for suitable candidates. Thus, job seekers now have additional criteria to fulfill in addition to simply stating their credentials, if they want to land that dream job in todays increasingly competitive environment.

What a Recruiter Wants

A job interview is a twofold process. On one hand, a potential employer will be gauging whether you have the capacity to competently fulfill the required role. The interview also allows for a company to form a well-rounded impression of whether a candidate has the personality and motivation to succeed in the particular industry for which they are interviewing. On the other hand, an interviewee has the opportunity to assess whether joining the organization is in line with their career goals, and is also given the chance to convince the hiring manager as to why they are the right fit for a job opening.

Perhaps the most baffling aspect of job hunting is figuring out exactly what recruiters are looking for. More importantly though, how can one get ahead of the pack to become that one outstanding candidate from many who actually lands the job?

The profile of an ideal employee differs from employer to employer. However, the basic tenets of having integrity, the drive to excel and the ability to learn quickly will generally get one noticed, especially if one has ambitions of climbing the corporate ladder. Even though there is no doubt that hard work, perseverance and diligence are essential qualities for success in any job, there are qualities outside of credentials and experience that will get the attention of employers – namely, attitude and mindset.

Businesses are facing various intense challenges in the current economy and market place. This increased competition has meant that companies now need to be lean and efficient. Thus, oftentimes they need employees who can do more than simply perform one particular function in the company. Favorable candidates are the ones who demonstrate creativity, commitment and passion to the job, showing that they are adaptable in a fast-paced working environment and are able to contribute to the business growth agenda in the industry for the long-run.

In summation, as a job seeker, your career survival and progression depends on how much you can contribute to an organization besides what is already specifically requested in the job description. The job interview is a window of opportunity in which you should be aiming to convince a potential employer that, not only can you fulfill the job requirements, but you can bring more to the table than what is being requested.

Chapter 2

Prepare Yourself!

Unless you are applying for a very niche type of job, it is to be expected that an employer will have no trouble finding someone who is equally qualified to fill the position and just as hard working, if not more so, that yourself. A job interview is your chance to shine, and you do not want to risk getting caught off guard by questions you cannot satisfactorily answer. So, as the old adage goes, "If you fail to prepare, you are preparing to fail". Do not go into an interview without making sure you are fully prepared in regard to the following:

1. Know your target audience and do your homework.

The audience in question refers to the organization in which you are seeking employment. Just as you should tailor fit your resume to suit each specific job you applying for, you should also approach each job interview with a clear mind and without holding too many assumptions. Different job openings require different strategies when going in for the interview. This is even more important if you are changing careers. You will need to find out what is specifically required of each position you will be interviewing for.

Too often, potential candidates end up jeopardizing their chances by coming across as having little to no idea about the role they are interviewing for or about the company itself. It is crucial that you thoroughly research the company who you will be interviewing with, as well as the latest happenings in the industry that you intend to work in. To show that you have taken the initiative to learn all you can about the position, company, and industry is a clear indication that you are genuinely keen to work for the company in question. It also tells the hiring manager that they have a candidate who is likely to be passionate about their work and who is serious about their career development.

Conversely, interviewers tend to consider a clueless candidate as not having enough interest in the job and thus, will not hesitate in dropping said candidate from the list of potentials right after the interview.

In the information age that we live in, a potential employer's information is normally just a Google search away. So, there is really no excuse for going into a job interview with zero background knowledge of an organization you want to work for.

2. Anticipate questions.

There are actually a number of standard interview questions hiring managers tend to swear by as a means of assessing candidates. To avoid the embarrassment of not being able to properly respond to a crucial question, it is vital to prepare – even if this is just in the form of mental notes – answers to some of the most common job interview questions. (More details on this subject in Chapter 3.)

3. A good first impression goes a long way.

Besides having knowledge of the potential employee and being able to answer questions appropriately, the way you carry yourself during an interview matters just as much in boosting your likability. So, it pays to give some thought to how you can make a good first impression. One of the simplest yet most effective ways to convey enthusiasm and confidence is with direct eye contact, a warm smile and a firm handshake. Be sure to keep this in mind and apply it when you greet the interviewer. Take time to also practice what you are going to say during the interview before attending.

4. Dress to impress.

Let's be honest; the moment you walk through a door, people will begin to formulate an impression of you based on how you look. Do not underestimate the importance of proper grooming, dressing appropriately and looking presentable. If you want to get the job, you have to look the part. Having done your research, you should know what the dress code is for the job and company you are going to interview for. Dress for an interview as if you were going to work. If you are interviewing for a job where the workplace allows t-shirt and jeans, play it safe and dress formally for the interview anyway. You can only assimilate into the corporate culture once you are hired.

Ready to Give it your Best Shot?

You have done your research on the potential employer, know the details of the business by heart, have the answers to common interview questions all carefully thought out, and the attire you will be wearing on that day selected. What could possibly go wrong? A job interview is a stressful situation, due to the fact that you will be placed in the spotlight to have your capabilities and personality assessed and judged.

As such, however confident you may be of your preparation pre-interview, do not rule out the possibility of nerves getting the better of you once you go before the interviewer.

According to Harvard psychologist and author of the bestseller on self-confidence, *Presence*, Amy Cuddy, job seekers are often less upset about not getting the job, but more about leaving an interview knowing that they could have done better. In other words, success in a stressful situation has more to do with walking away without regrets because you did your best, rather than getting a positive outcome.

Taking that into account, the final step of your preparation is to work on what Cuddy calls, "a presence" – the ability to fully and confidently represent yourself in a challenging situation. On the day of the interview, arrive at least 30 minutes earlier then the scheduled interview start time, and take a while for the following self-confidence boosters and to calm yourself:

1. Accept that you could be nervous.

No matter how well prepared you are to face a challenge, there may be times when it is practically impossible to curb the feeling of panic from rising. It should be understood that the nervousness you feel going into a job interview is a normal reaction to what many would perceive to be a trying situation. This acceptance can make you more aware of your emotional state when entering the interview, and minimize the frustration if things do not go as planned, so that you can accept your slip-ups as lessons learned.

2. Remind yourself of what you stand for.

What normally triggers anxiety during a job interview is the subconscious fear that you are perceived as not good enough. Cuddy suggests a small exercise of self-affirmation before going into a job interview – take a moment to write down a core value that is meaningful to you, followed by a time when that value came into play. What do you stand for? It could be your discipline that has led to academic achievements (graduated top of the class), a personal accomplishment brought on by patience and determination (having travelled the continent on your own earnings), or your career success for being diligent (having a good track record in the past jobs you have held).

This exercise may not seem like much, but it will remind you of and reaffirm what you as a unique individual have to bring to the table, and that you should believe in yourself. Self-affirmations, Cuddy writes, are "a way of grounding ourselves in the truth of our own stories. It makes us feel less dependent on the approval of others and even comfortable with their disapproval, if that's what we get."

3. Just breathe.

After you have affirmed yourself, take a moment to control your breath. Here is a simple yoga breathing exercise to calm your nerves: inhale to the count of 4, hold your breath for a count of 7, and exhale to the count of 8. Repeat this exercise 3-5 times, and wait patiently for your name to be called.

4. Mind your body language.

Actions of the physical body create a thought reaction, which in turn creates an emotional reaction that affects behavior. See how the body, mind and feelings are in constant conversation with one another? We cannot help how we feel, and it can be difficult controlling the thoughts that creep into our minds. However, we can immediately change what we do with our body.

Developing powerful body language is important in feeling more confident. Body language that conveys power and self-assurance is expansive and open; you occupy space by holding your arms and legs away from the body. When you are called into the interview seat, sit upright and fill your chair. Do not slouch or sit on the edge, and refrain from twiddling your thumbs or shaking your legs – that is a sure giveaway that you are nervous!

Chapter 3

The Art of the Answer

If you feel apprehensive at the thought of a job interview, bear in mind that it is essentially a formal meeting for a potential employer to further assess your suitability for a job. The questions you are bound to be asked during a job interview are intended to evaluate your professionalism in relation to an open position.

Nevertheless, it helps to be prepared with replies for commonly asked interview questions, and enlist the help of a more experienced friend to aid you with by doing a rehearsal. By the time you walk in for the interview, you should be confident in answering questions relating to your interest in the position, as well as your most notable achievements, strengths, weaknesses and career goals in the near future.

Here is a simple cheat sheet to a dozen common interview questions and tips on how to handle them. Bear in mind there is no one-size-fits-all answers, and it would be more advantageous not to have a script of how to response. You may just get caught off guard if the interviewer decided to throw in an odd question.

1. "Tell me about yourself."

A classic ice-breaker that normally starts off an interview. To stumble on this question is to be off to a bad start. When asked to talk about yourself in a job interview, it is not a cue to go into your life story! Talk about your professional history, how you started in the industry, past work experiences, what you have learned thus far, and conclude with what garnered your interest in this specific job opportunity. Keep you answer succinct and to the point, but most importantly, keep it relevant to the job.

2. "What is your greatest strength?"

This should be a fairly straight forward question, and if you have done your research on the company, you should know what strengths you have which they are likely to value. This is your opportunity to shine, so make it work to your advantage! Highlight your biggest strength that is crucial to the position. If you have any relevant achievements in the past due to this trait, make brief mention of it. For instance, if you know the job is deadline-centric, you can say that punctuality is your greatest strength and you have a consistent track record of meeting deadlines in your previous job. Take care to strike a balance between modesty and flaunting your capabilities; you do not want to come across as a braggart.

3. "Give an example of a difficult work situation and what you did to overcome it."

This is a common interview question that candidates often struggle to answer. So, be sure you have a "success story" prepared. A good answer is a specific example which illustrates how you dealt with a problem successfully, and also reflects how you exhibit the skills and strengths required by the job you are being interviewed for. You can use the S.T.A.R. method to structure your answer (Situation, Task, Action, Response). A pitfall to be careful of here is to not bash anyone in your success story, even if there really was someone at fault. For example, there is no need to point out that the problem you are talking about was caused by your previous boss's lack of forethought, or a pesky customer – just focus on the situation and the solution you provided.

4. "What is your greatest weakness?"

Candidates often feel intimidated and try to sidestep the question about their weakness, fearing that it will jeopardize their chances. In actual fact, the question is meant to reflect your self-awareness and show that you have the ability to take action in improving yourself. Refrain from responding with the cliché, "I'm a perfectionist" or "My strength is also my weakness" – these are dead giveaways that you are attempting to dodge the question by covering up your actual weakness. A sensible way to answer would be to choose a weakness that is not a core competency of the job in question, and then make a brief mention of efforts you are making to overcome it.

5. "What is your greatest accomplishment?"

A question about your accomplishments can be handled in the same manner as a¥ question about your greatest strength. Pick an accomplishment that highlights qualities which are desirable for the job you are interviewing for, and also shows that you are passionate about the work you do. Even experienced candidates often make the mistake of thinking their accomplishments are too small to tout. In reality, a small accomplishment that is in line with company's values will make more of an impact than a bigger, but irrelevant one. For example, if you are interviewing for the position of project manager, it would be better to mention having zero missed deadlines in a year as an accomplishment, than saying you once won a salesperson of the year award.

6. "Where do you see yourself in 5 years?"

Perhaps the most intimidating and tricky question. You want to answer in a manner that shows you are ambitious, but also realistic enough that your head is not in the clouds. Let you answer demonstrate your level of commitment to the job you are being interviewed for, then outline a reasonable growth strategy that ties in with the needs of the company. The bottom line is you want to emphasize that you are serious about your career aspirations, and you have interest in a long-term career in this company. Steer clear of saying anything that implies the company or job in question is just a stepping stone to your true ambitions; companies are looking to hire individuals who are committed to the growth of their organization. Saying that you want to be the CEO in the next five years, or telling the recruiter "I want to be in your position" are almost guaranteed to ruin your chances of getting the job.

7. "Why did you leave your last job?" / "Why are you thinking of leaving your current job?"

You may be changing jobs for various personal reasons. The golden rule when asked at a job interview is to refrain from discussing any sort of problems, conflicts or complains regarding your previous employment. It will only reflect badly on your character. Your answer should focus on constructive career-related reasons, such as seeking new challenges and opportunities for growth. Be sure to reference a specific characteristic this company has that will benefit your career in a way your previous job did not.

Avoid saying something along the lines of "It's time for a career change, because I am tired of doing the same thing. So, I'd like to try my hand at the job you are offering." Such a statement implies that you are taking the opportunity offered lightly. Another no-no reason for leaving your previous job is to complain about low pay and lack of incentives.

Do not lie if you were terminated; be honest about it and explain what you have learned from the experience. The interviewer is more likely to know that you are aware of your mistakes and are able to do something about it. Termination due to reasons beyond your control, such as company downsizing or economic downturn, are acceptable reasons for leaving a job.

8. "Why do you want to work for us?" / "What interests you about this job?"

When this question comes up, the hiring manager is trying to gauge your underlying motive for wanting the job. Are you just in it for the money? Or are you genuinely interested in growing a career with their organization? Your answer should focus on what you are passionate about, and how this job offer allows you to fulfill that. Show how your skills and strengths fulfill the company's needs and accommodate your career goals. You may throw in a dose of flattery ("Company X is one of the industry leaders."), but do not go overboard or you will come across as sycophantic.

The key is to focus on the substance of the role being offered and how it interests you. Do not mention the salary, incentives or other personal benefits not related to the job. You could give off the impression of taking on the job as a means to an end, and no employer will be willing to invest in an employee who will only be around for a few months. Oh, and saying "Because I need the money" is a surefire way to get dropped for consideration before the interview ends.

9. "Why should we hire you?"

Here is another great opportunity to separate yourself from the rest and show what you can bring to the company. Your answer should be specific; do not say why you want the job, but elaborate on why you are a perfect fit for the job. If you have done your homework ahead of time, you should be aware of what the company's specific needs are and be able to leverage that to your advantage. You want to show that you are knowledgeable about the company and the industry, and that you have the unique set of qualities required to fill these specific needs.

10. "What do you know about our company?"

The interviewer is not going to want to hear you state memorized facts about their company; they are already well aware of these facts. They want to see if you have a general understanding of what their business is all about. What makes the company different from its competitors? What is it known for and what does it stand for? Has it been in the news lately? What are their recent accomplishments in the industry? A lack of knowledge will make the interviewer wonder how interested you really are in working for them.

11. "What's most important to you in a new position?"

This question is asked as a way for the interviewer to understand your career goals and whether the job offer fulfills them. If you are looking for a job with a lot of flexibility where you can mostly work solo, you would not be a right fit if the job offer requires a lot of team work and collaboration. Answer this question candidly and specifically. If you are looking for a job with specific challenges and the prospect for growth, mention it, but refrain from subjects of salary and compensation.

12. "Do you have any questions?"

Approximately 80% of candidates respond to this question with, "No, I think you have covered everything." Often, one of the mistakes potential candidates make during a job interview is to not ask the interviewer questions when presented the opportunity.

Nothing indicates that one is serious about their career and a job offer more than demonstrating a desire to learn beyond what they already know. Here are some smart questions you may want to ask, if the answers have not already been made apparent during the interview:

- What are the growth prospects in the organization?

- What does it take to be successful in this company?

- What are the challenges that someone in this role should anticipate?

- Can you tell me more about the corporate culture here?

- If offered the position, what would be the most important things you would like to see me accomplish in the first 30, 60 and 90 days of my employment?

- Can you give me some examples of where team work and collaborations is necessary/possible in the company?

For a thorough list of interview questions you should prepare for before attending an interview, see "Chapter 6: More Interview Questions You Should Prepare For".

Chapter 4

The Slippery Slope

Imagine this: you go into the interview well-prepared and everything is going smoothly. Then, just as you are about to end things on a triumphant note, the interviewer suddenly asks you how many times heavier than a mouse an elephant is. Since 2015 onwards, such brainteaser questions – also known as a curveball question – have slowly become a staple in job interviews, leaving job candidates dumbfounded.

Fortunately, there is no need for you to get these odd questions right, because there really is no right or wrong answer. Rather, it is an opportunity for the employer to observe the candidate's thought process, how they perform under pressure and think on the spot. In this chapter, you will examine half a dozen of the most common types of curveball questions, and what they are actually intended to assess. By preparing you will be less likely to get caught off guard in the event that the interviewer decides to throw you one. Also addressed here is another of the biggest interview worries: should you discuss salary and compensation during a job interview?

1. "How much would you charge to wash all of the windows in town?"

Questions like this are designed to see how quickly you are able to think on your feet and what goes through your head. Will you try to estimate how many windows there are in town? Will you decide on a fixed price per window? Or will you estimate how long it takes to clean all windows and charge by the hour? Bear in mind there is not right or wrong answer. What matters are how you justified you answer, as the interviewer is interested in hearing the rationale behind your thought process.

2. "Explain a database (or any concept/ technical term/process) to an eight-year-old."

You may get this type of question if you are interviewing for a job that deals heavily with industry-specific concepts and processes. If you will be interacting with clients, it is crucial to be able to simplify complicated concepts and explain them in plain English. This question is to gauge how well you can translate tech speak for the comprehension of the layperson.

3. "Describe the color red to someone who is blind."

How creative and sensitive are you? How well are you able to express abstract ideas and think outside the box? This question is a test of your wits and your insight. If you are able to train yourself to look at things from multiple angles, you should have no problem with this kind of question.

4. "If you have 1,000 emails in your inbox but enough time to only answer 300 of them, how would you choose?"

This question is deceptively easy; it probes at how organized you are and how well you prioritize when under pressure. The best answer is based on common sense: you would reply to emails from your biggest client, the boss, or anything time-sensitive, while everything else can wait.

5. "Tell me about a time when you had a disagreement with a colleague (or manager/customer). How was it resolved?"

This can be considered a sneaky variation of the classic question, "Why did you leave your last job?" or "Why are you thinking of leaving your current job?". The same rules of how to respond apply here; be careful not to bad mouth anyone. Give an example of a situation and focus on how the matter was resolved. Your answer should show that you are not afraid of conflict, and that you are mature enough to not take things personally in a professional situation.

6. "What did you have for breakfast/lunch/dinner?"

As odd as it may sound, such seemingly meaningless questions do get asked from time to time, although the subject of the question may vary. If this question sounds like it has nothing to do with the job you are being interviewed for, you are most likely right. In organizations that have a tight-knit corporate culture, such as places where lunches are supplied by a cafeteria or caterer, your answer to this question will help the interviewer see if you will fit in. There is no better way to answer this than to just be yourself. It may not be that big of a deal, and is unlikely to affect your qualifications for the job. On the off-chance it it does, it is probably better that you find a job somewhere else where you fit in better than to work in an environment that doesn't suit you.

Should You Discuss Salary?

Perhaps the trickiest question during an interview – especially for the first-time job seeker – is salary expectations. When it comes to discussing compensation, job seekers are advised to tread carefully.

Normally, a salary range will be indicated on the job advertisement. If there is none, or if it is indicated that "salary is negotiable", a job seeker should never be the one to bring up questions about compensation. Your focus for the interview should be to show that you are genuinely interested in the job itself, and sell your skills, experiences and achievements. The discussion regarding salary is best left aside until you are offered the position.

You may or may not get asked about how much you are expecting to get paid during a job interview, but if the question comes up, it is best to avoid mentioning a specific number. At worst, you may give off the impression of being too demanding, focusing more on the money than being sincerely interest in the job. Instead, state a realistic range which is around how much someone with your qualifications and experience stands to earn, and politely redirect the question back to the interviewer by asking for their suggestion of what they believe to be a fair compensation for the position.

If you believe you are entitled to a higher salary than what is offered, for whatever reason, negotiate at your own risk and get ready to justify the amount you are asking for!

Chapter 5

The Worst Things You Can Do

By now, you should feel confident and well-prepared for any upcoming job interview. In addition to all the crucial elements that have been covered, here are 12 more often overlooked factors, some of which are minor issues and others absolute no-nos, that could easily ruin your chances of landing your dream job. After all, an interview is the last chance you will get to convince an employer why you are the best fit for their company, so make this crucial opportunity count.

1. Showing up late.

If you arrive for an interview later than the appointed time, you are already off to a bad start. Being punctual should be at the top of the list when it comes to making a good first impression.

2. Get caught lying.

A definite guarantee that you will not get the job is to lie during the job interview. If you are going to make a bold claim or state something that is not true, seriously think about your chances of getting away with it. Companies run background checks on potential hires. Whether it is about your credentials, accomplishments or your work history, honesty will usually be the best policy.

3. Forgetting common courtesy.

Did you greet the interviewer politely with a smile and a firm handshake? When the interview ended did you give another handshake and thank the interviewer for their time? If you did not do any of those, do not be surprised if you do not hear back from the potential employer again. Interviewers gather clues about candidates based on whether they are punctual, how they are dressed, the eye contact they make and the words they use. A minor slip up, such not maintaining basic manners, can cost you dearly.

4. Straying too far from a question.

As questions are being asked, keep your answers to the point and relevant to the context of the interview. It also helps to provide specific examples to support your answers, such as talking about a scenario that happened in the past to illustrate your skills and accomplishments. The important thing to remember is to keep things directly related to the questions being asked and not go off topic.

5. Inappropriate humor.

Be confident, but avoid cracking jokes unnecessarily or saying things probably best left unsaid. A little touch of humor could work in your favor, provided that it is appropriate to the context of the interview. You do not need to be funny, especially when it is at the expense of appropriateness and formality. The last thing you want is for the hiring manager to think you are not serious about the job opportunity.

6. Getting personal.

A job interview is a formal meeting to assess if you are the right fit for a job. Everything in your personal life, your subjective opinions and how you are feeling should be left outside the door, and not be brought up during the interview.

7. Appearing arrogant and entitled.

No one owes you a job; you have to earn the opportunity. If you really are the right candidate for the job, your credentials and professionalism will speak for itself. You appear full of yourself if you make inflated claims about your qualifications, bad mouth previous employers or make assumptions about the job role.

8. Not appearing attentive.

It goes without saying that you should give 101% of your attention to the interviewer and respond to questions accordingly. Not smiling, playing with something on the table, bad posture, no eye contact, and fidgeting too much are behaviors indicating you are not paying attention. Additionally, checking your phone or answering calls are almost definitely job interview deal breakers.

9. Mind your language.

Keep your language formal and professional. Avoid cursing, profanity and "cute" remarks ("My wife wants me to get this job"); you may think you are being witty and funny, but the interviewer will take it as rude and a lack of professionalism. The same thing should apply to your tone of speech. That means no speaking loudly or remarks which could be perceived as impolite.

10. Saying more than you have to.

Shakespeare once said that "Brevity is the soul of wit", and he is absolutely right. So, answer whatever is asked of you by the interviewer and avoid rambling on.

11. Bringing an entourage.

You are the one who will be interviewed; there is no need for any pomp and pageantry. Family members, friends and significant others – no matter how well-meaning they might be – should not accompany you when you are going for a job interview. There have even been extreme cases of people bringing their pets along - do not do that.

12. Ask when the interview will end.

Nothing says "I don't care about this job and I am just wasting your time" like asking the interviewer how long the interview will be, or when will it end. You will also be doing just as much damage by constantly looking at your watch. When you are called in for a job interview, you are expected to make time for it, if you really want to get the job.

Chapter 6

100 More Interview Questions You Should Prepare For

In Chapter 3, "The Art of the Answer", we took a detailed look at some of the questions you may well be asked in an interview and the kinds of answer the interviewer is likely to be looking for. In this chapter I'll be offering you more examples of the types of questions an interviewer may well ask, broken down into the various areas of questioning. While you may not be asked all of these questions, and while the wording of the questions you are asked may be slightly different, being well-prepared to answer these questions will definitely be of value to you. Have a good think about what an interviewer is likely to be looking for when answering these questions and prepare your responses accordingly. Refer back to Chapter 3 if you're not sure of the kind of answer which may be best.

The Basics

1. Tell us about yourself.

2. What do you consider to be your main strengths?

3. What do you consider to be your weaknesses?

4. Why did you apply for the position?/Why do you want this job?

5. What attracted you to apply for a position in this company in particular?

6. Why should we hire you?

7. What did you find most challenging in your previous job?

8. Where do you see yourself five years from now in regard to your career?

9. Tell us about your ideal company.

10. When were you most satisfied in your work-life?

11. What makes you a better fit for the position compared to other candidates?

12. What were your main responsibilities in your previous position?

13. Why are you leaving your present company?

14. What do you know about the industry we are involved in?

15. Tell us a little about what you know about our company?

16. Are you willing to relocate if required?

17. Are there any questions you'd like to ask us?

Questions related to your personality

18. Tell us about the last project you led. What was the outcome of the project?

19. What's an an example of a time that you felt you went above and beyond what was expected in terms of your work life?

20. Describe a time when your work was criticized? How did you deal with this criticism?

21. Have you had experience of being on a team where someone was not pulling their weight? How did you deal with the situation?

22. Tell me about a time when you had to give someone negative feedback. How did you deal with the situation?

23. What has been your biggest regret, and what did you learn from it?

24. How do you handle working with people who you don't get along with?

25. If your supervisor asked you to do something that you didn't agree with, how would you deal with the situation?

26. When do you consider to be the most difficult period in your life? How did you get through this period?

27. Give us an example of a time when you made a mistake. How did you overcome it?

28. Tell us about a time where you had to deal with some form of conflict at work.

29. If you were attending a business lunch and the order you received wasn't quite what you expected, what would you do?

30. If you found out that your company was in some way doing something not strictly legal, how would you deal with this issue?

31. Have you ever had any assignments which were too difficult for you? If so, how did you deal with the issue?

32. What's the most difficult decision you've made in the last few years and how did you come to this decision?

33. Describe how you would handle a situation if you were required to finish multiple tasks by the end of the day, and there was no conceivable way that you could finish them all. How would you prioritize these tasks?

Questions related to Salary

34. What is the salary that you are currently seeking?

35. What's your history interns of salary in your previous positions?

36. If I were to give you the salary you requested but asked you to write your own job description for the coming year, what would you write?

Questions related to your career development

37. What are your goals in terms of you career development over the next year or so?

38. How do you plan to improve yourself in the coming months?

39. What kind of goals would you envisage yourself working towards if you were to be offered this job?

40. If I were to ask your last supervisor to provide details of where you could benefit from you

additional training or experience, what do you

think they would recommend?

Questions related to making an initial impact on the job

41. If you were to be offered this job, how would you go about establishing your credibility quickly within the team you would be a part of?

42. How long do you feel it would take for you to make a significant contribution to the work we do here?

43. What do you imagine you might be doing in the first 30 days of joining this company?

44. If offered the position, what would be your strategy for the first 90 days of your new work life with us here?

More questions related to your personality

45. Describe your work style, as you see it.

46. Describe your ideal working environment and why this environment appeals to you.

47. What do you prefer in terms of a company's work culture -- a structured or more autonomous environment?

48. Give examples of ideas you've had and successfully managed to implement.

49. What techniques and tools do you use to keep yourself organized? How effective do you feel you are at doing this?

50. If you had to choose, do you consider yourself more of a big-picture person or a detail-oriented person?

51. Tell me about the achievement you are most proud of.

52. Which of your managers were you most fond of and why?

53. What's your opinion of your previous boss?

54. Has there been a person in your work life who you feel really made a difference?

55. What kind of personality types do you work best with and why?

56. What achievement in your life are you most proud of?

57. What do you most like to do if money and time weren't an obstacle?

58. What are your lifelong dreams and have you moved towards their achievement?

59. What do you ultimately want to achieve in your life? What kind of person do you want to become?

60. What is your personal mission statement and what are your daily focus points?

61. What are three positive things that you would expect your last boss might say about you?

62. What might your last boss say about you that would be negative?

63. What three adjectives do you think your friends would use to describe your personality?

64. What are three positive character traits you don't feel you currently have? How are you working to improve in these areas?

65. If you were interviewing someone for this position, what personality traits would you look for?

66. Which five words do you feel best describe your character?

67. Who has had the biggest impact on your career and how?

68. What is your greatest fear for the future?

69. What is your biggest regret thus far in your life and why?

70. What do you consider to be the most important thing you learned in school?

71. Why did you choose to study the subject you studied at University?

72. What will you miss about your current job after you leave?

73. What would you consider to be your greatest achievement in terms of your personal life?

74. What are the qualities of a good leader and of a bad leader?

75. Do you think a leader should be feared or liked by their subordinates?

76. How do you feel about being told "no" when t comes to your work life?

77. How would you feel about having a boss who knows less than you?

78. What do you think of me as an interviewer?

79. Tell me one thing about yourself that you don't think I should know.

80. How would you define the difference between good and great.

81. What kind of car would you most like to drive and why?

82. If you could be anywhere in the world right now, where would you chose to be and why?

83. What's the last book you read? How was it?

84. What magazines do you regularly read?

85. What's the best movie you've seen in the last year or so? Briefly describe the plot.

86. What would you do if you were to win the lottery?

87. Who are your role-models?

88. Who was your childhood hero?

89. What kinds of activities do you consider most enjoyable?

90. What do you do like to do in your spare time?

91. What is one of your best favorite memories from your childhood?

Typical Brainteasers

92. If you could choose one superhero power, what would it be and why?

93. If you could get rid of any one of the US states, which one would you get rid of and why?

94. With your eyes closed, tell me step-by-step how to tie my shoes.

95. Tell me 10 ways to use a pencil other than writing.

96. Sell me this pencil.

97. If you were an animal, which one would you want to be?

98. Why is there fuzz on a tennis ball?

99. How many times do a clock's hands overlap in a day?

100.How would you weigh a plane without scales?

<u>Conclusion</u>

As you have no doubt seen, there are many factors involved when it comes to successfully interviewing for a job, and things are perhaps not as simple now as they may have been in the past. However, by following the guidelines outlined in this book, you will be well on your way to interviewing well and one step closer to your dream job!

Good luck!

A message from the author, Steve Gold

To show my appreciation for your support, Id like to offer you the following:

FREE BONUS!

As a free bonus, I've included a preview of one of my other best-selling books directly after this section. Enjoy!

ALSO...

Be sure to check out my other books. Scroll to the back of this book for a list of other books written by me, along with download links.

Finally, if you enjoyed this book, **please** take the time to post a review on Amazon. It will only take a couple of minutes and I'd be extremely grateful for your support.

Thank you again for your support.

Steve Gold

FREE BONUS!: Preview Of "Resume - How To Write A Resume Which Will Get You Hired In 2016"!

If you enjoyed this book, I have a little bonus for you; a preview of one of my other books "Resume - How To Write A Resume Which Will Get You Hired In 2016".

With technology changing the way we live and work, there's no doubt job hunting is no longer the same as it was just a few years ago. Even so, writing a winning resume will significantly increase your chances of getting invited for an interview.

In this concise guide, you will learn about the "dos and don'ts" of great resume writing. The tips and tricks in this book are specifically geared towards helping you land a job in the present-day job market. With some modern additions to your resume, you can give yourself the competitive edge which may well be the all important deciding factor in whether or not you land that dream job!

Introduction

A resume is the most important self-advertising tool at an individual's disposal when it comes to finding a job. Before you even get the opportunity to impress a hiring manager with your wonderful personality and people skills in an interview, your résumé will need to make a good first impression and stand up to the scrutiny of a perspective employer. Your resume acts as the key which will (or will not) unlock the door and grant you access to tout your qualifications and your suitability for a particular job position in person.

Due to the numerous methods available when it comes to advertising job openings in various channels today, it is easy for employers to get overwhelmed with more applications than they have the time to go through thoroughly. That means for every vacancy you apply for, you will most likely be competing against tens, hundreds, maybe even thousands of other job-seekers who share similar credentials, skills and experience to yourself.

With technology changing the way we live and work, there is no doubt job hunting is no longer the same as it was just a few years ago. Even so, writing a winning résumé will still make all the difference in getting you noticed by potential employers. This, in turn, will significantly increase your chances of getting a call back for an interview.

In this concise guide, you will learn about the "dos and don'ts" of great resume writing, and these tips and tricks are specifically geared towards finding a job in the present time. Even if you are an old hand at job hunting, you will also find helpful hints on how to tweak your resume so as to keep up with current trends.

With some modern additions to your resume, you can give yourself the competitive edge which may well be the all important deciding factor to whether or not you land that dream job!

Chapter 1

Job Hunting: Then vs. Now

It is an understatement to say that competition in the job market today is tougher than ever before. For the inexperienced job seeker, even the application process can be daunting, especially when one gets no reply or status update after sending out numerous applications.

For the experienced candidate looking for a career change, it can be confusing trying figure out how to get that all important advantage with recruiters. After all, of the many candidates competing for open positions, a tiny handful of hopefuls will get a call back for an interview, and most likely only one person will get hired in the end.

Significant shifts in hiring practices and job hunting can be attributed to an obvious source: technology. Specifically, the ubiquity of the internet and mobile technology in the 21st century is changing the way talent is discovered and recruited.

According to a late 2015 report – jointly produced by consulting firm, Boston Consulting Group, and research organization, Recruit Works Institute – the internet has become the primary channel for job searching. The report findings were gathered by surveying over 13,000 job seekers from 13 countries in order to establish a global view of the latest processes involved in searching for a job. It was revealed that approximately 55% of respondents sought new job opportunities online through job posting websites, compared to only 36% who consulted paper media and 33% who relied on referrals from friends and family.

However, the internet is breaking the recruitment mould in more than one way. While candidates and recruiters typically turn to job posting websites as a platform, social media and mobile applications are increasingly playing a pivotal role in people getting hired. This is hardly surprising, because we live in an era where people rely on social media and mobile devices to stay connected. Hence, several job search websites are already making headway by developing their own mobile apps, as an extension of their services, to make job postings accessible on handheld devices.

There is also a noticeable trend of employers turning to social media for recruitment, especially on professional network, LinkedIn. This is due in large part to the fact that a social media page gives a recruiter more insight into a candidate than just a resume accompanied by a cover letter.

Death of the Traditional Resume

With online job hunting and recruiting becoming the norm, the personnel in charge of hiring are getting bombarded with a larger than usual number of applications. TheLadders, an American-based company providing online job search services, found in a 2015 study that recruiters generally spend only six seconds reviewing each individual resume before deciding if the candidate is worth further consideration. That's assuming that your resume even gets reviewed by a human! Some companies, especially bigger corporations, employ automated tracking systems to screen through resumes. The same study also indicated that resumes which are deemed difficult to read at first glance, due to poor visual presentation, will be given even less time.

What this means for job seekers is that your resume has to be, not only professionally written, but also easy on the recruiters' eyes and mind in terms of it's visual presentation. It has to grab the hiring manager's attention from the moment it's viewed. Gone are the days where a neatly typed formal document on a white sheet will suffice. The modernized resume must equally showcase your individuality just as it touts your job qualifications.

So, when tailoring your resume for the next job you plan on applying for, it is worth remembering that you may only have six seconds to impress the person who's going to be receiving you resume. Make every word and visual element count!

In a nutshell, an outstanding resume in the modern age should meet the following criteria:

- Visually well presented for easy reading

- Eye-catching in design

- Written in a formal and professional manner

- Free of errors and spelling mistakes

- Contains words that "sell" you as a candidate (also known as "keywords" or "buzzwords")

- Relevant to the job being applied for

- Highlights a candidates qualifications in clear and concise sentences

- Makes it easy for the candidate to be contacted (email address, telephone number)

- Represents your individual professional brand

Take note of these key elements and keep them in mind when writing your resume. If you already have a written resume, run through the checklist above and see how it stacks up. Each of these points will be addressed in greater detail in subsequent chapters, and you will be guided on how to make each of them work for you in your job applications.

Check out the rest of "Resume - How To Write A Resume Which Will Get You Hired In 2016" on Amazon.

Check Out My Other Books!

Elon Musk - The Biography Of A Modern Day Renaissance Man

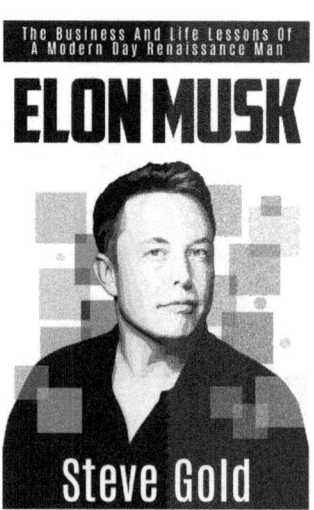

Elon Musk - The Business & Life Lessons Of A Modern Day Renaissance Man

Warren Buffett - The Business And Life Lessons Of An Investment Genius, Magnate And Philanthropist

Steve Jobs - The Biography & Lessons Of The Mastermind Behind Apple

Management - Achieve Management Excellence & World Class Leadership Skills In 7 Simple Steps

Sales - Easily Sell Anything To Anyone & Achieve Sales Excellence In 7 Simple Steps

Arduino - Getting Started With Arduino: The Ultimate Beginner's Guide

(If the links do not work, for whatever reason, you can simply search for these titles on the Amazon to find them. All books available as ebooks or printed books)